Magical Mudras

An Earth Lodge Pocket Guide to Using
Mudras for Health and Manifestation

MAYA COINTREAU

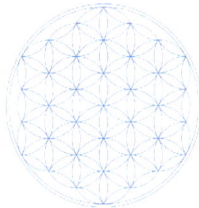

An Earth Lodge Publication
Roxbury, CT, USA

Also by Maya Cointreau

How Can You Use Mudras?

Mudras have benefits for both body and mind, many of which continue to be studied and validated by scientific research. One recent study showed that they have the same effect on the brain as language: when you use a mudra, you are activating a specific thought or intent, and that thought carries energy, working like a radio signal to communicate with all the energy around you: sending your desire out into the Universe, to God, to All that IS, for fulfillment and manifestation.

Mudras can be formed during meditation, while watching TV or brushing your teeth. Mudras can be used in your artwork to portray hidden meaning or intent.

This book is meant to be a simple guide to the mudras, making it easier to reference them on the fly in a joyful and colorful way. Have fun with the mudras in this book. Look at them when the mood strikes you, or use them every day. Above all: *enjoy them!*

What is a Mudra?

Mudras are symbolic hand gestures or positions used throughout the world in spiritual and daily practice. Buddhist monks and Indian yogis use mudras to empower their meditations; Hindu and Buddhist statuary use mudras to show the intent of the portrayed divine being; Christian paintings of Jesus and other holy figures often show the hands in various mudras, or gestures. Mudras influence the energy flowing through your cells, the emotions affecting your thoughts, and help open the way to enlightenment.

There are literally hundreds of symbolic gestures in the world: this book focuses primarily upon some of the more popular eastern mudras of the Buddha and those used in yogic exercises. There are 108 mudras used in Tantric yoga alone, and well over two hundred used in Indian classical dance. They are used throughout the martial arts to help harness universal source energy, or Qi, for the user.

The **Abhaya,** or **Abhayaprada,** mudra shows fearlessness and courage. It is a friendly, calming gesture used to pacify others and show that you come in peace. Hold your hand at shoulder level with the palm facing outwards.

The **Ahamkara** mudra is also used to combat fear and is believed to raise self-confidence. Most westerners know it well as the "All OK" symbol. Bend your middle finger and place your thumb its second phalanx, keeping your other three fingers held straight up.

The **Akash** Mudra, or sky posture, connects your heart chakra with Source energy. Very healing, it calms angry fire energy and opens you to the soothing influence of the sky, to the quietude of spirit. Connect the tips of your thumb and middle finger while keeping your other fingers held straight.

The **Apaan** mudra grounds excess energy. It soothes the mind and connects you to Mother Earth. It is interesting to note that many children make this mudra in play, and indeed it is a very good mudra for anyone who has issues with concentration of hyperactivity. Connect the tips of your thumb, middle and ring fingers and extend your pinky and index finger.

The **Buddha** mudra is a receptive gesture where you rest one open palm inside the other with your thumb tips connected. If you are a man, rest your right hand on top; if you are a woman, the left goes on top. Use this gesture to show the universe your gratitude and that you are open to receiving.

The **Buddhasramana** mudra is used to show one's renunciation of worldly attachments and matters. Material concerns are of no import. The ascetic relinquishes such things so that he may pursue the path of enlightenment and seeks compassion and upliftment for all living beings. The hand is held up at shoulder level, flat and relaxed with the palm up and the fingers pointing away from the body.

The **Bhudi** balances your ether and earth elements, helping you connect your body and spirit. It is often used to enhance communication, intuition and psychic abilities. Touch the tips of your thumb and pinky together and extend the three middle fingers

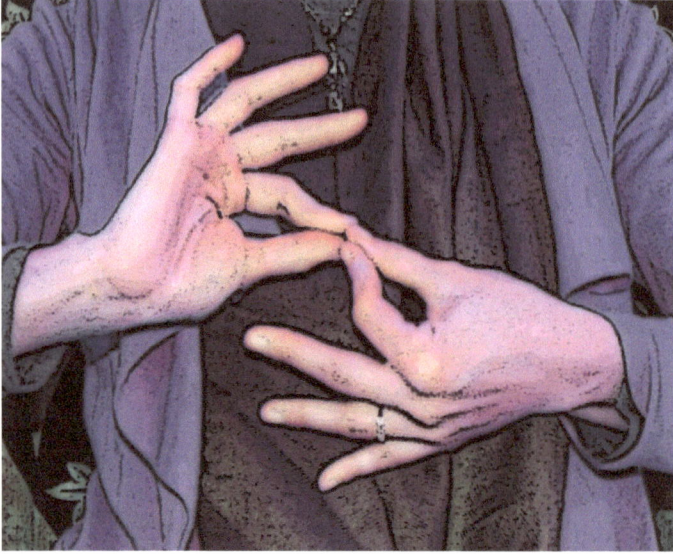

The **Dharmachakra** Mudra symbolizes the moment that the Enlightened Buddha began teaching in Deer Park, the first teaching. It is a gesture that connects one to the eternal teachings and records of Source, of God, and that connects one to Buddha and the ascended Masters. Hold your hands at heart level, with the left palm facing your body and your right palm facing outwards, and connect your thumbs and index fingertips while extending your other fingers. Now you are turning the Wheel of Dharma, the wheel of truth and enlightenment, and receiving directly from Source.

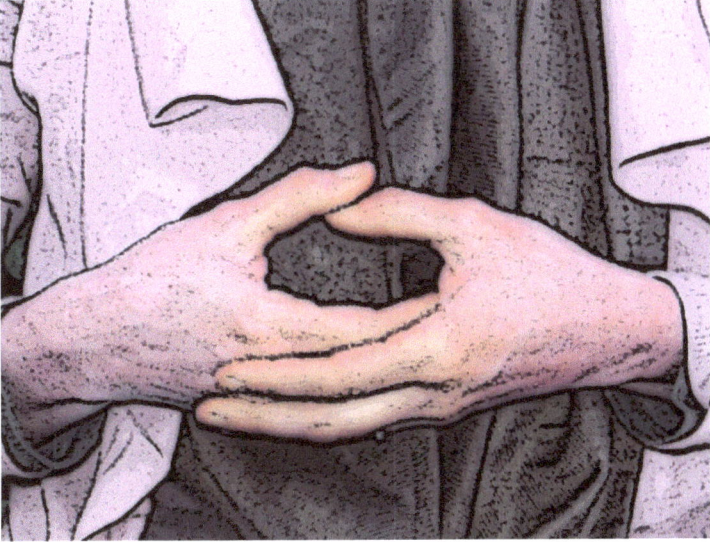

The **Dhyana,** or **Samadhi,** mudra is perhaps one of the most common hand positions used during meditation and in representations of Buddha. Use your hands to create a bowl shape, with your thumbs touching to form a triangle or a circle, or to rest on the palms. This gesture shows peace and balance.

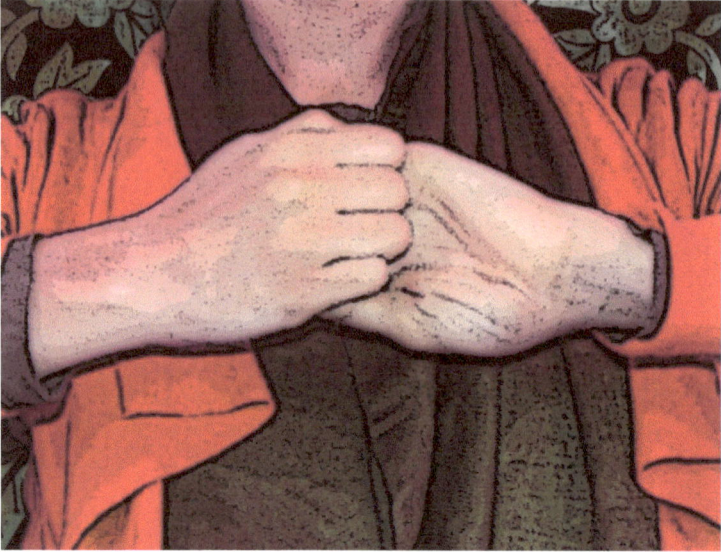

The **Ganesha** mudra is used to open the heart and throat chakras, remove obstacles and bring blessings into your life, invoking the wisdom and power of Ganesha, the elephant god. At chest level, grasp your right hand in the left, locking them together and applying gentle pressure in opposite directions as you breathe in. Do this 5-10 times, then reverse the palms and repeat.

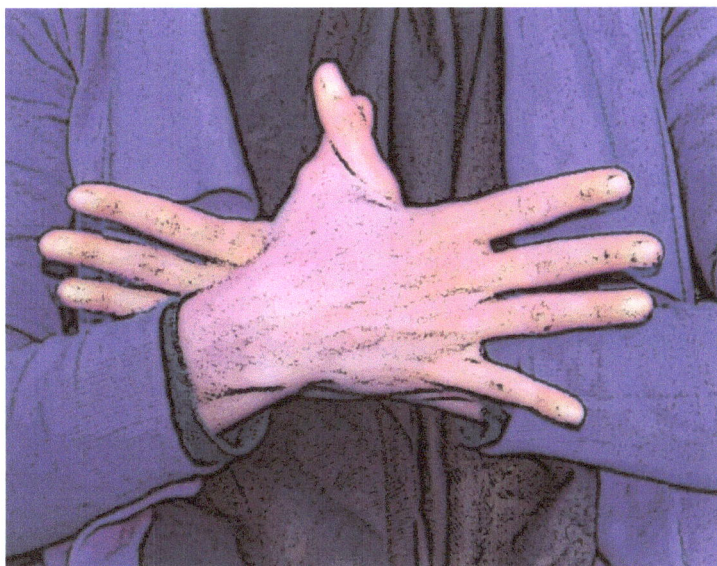

The **Garuda** mudra is protective and freeing. Associated with the strength of the phoenix-like Garuda from Hindu and Buddhist lore, this gesture helps release anger and stress. Excess energy accumulated throughout the day can be easily dispersed using this mudra, allowing you to return to joy and live in the moment. Place your hands at your solar plexus, one over the other and interlock your thumbs. Spread your fingers open and get ready to take flight!

The **Gyan** mudra is believed to increase memory and mental faculties, and is therefore considered a gesture of learning. Use this mudra when you are reading or in class to improve retention, or use it to benefit your meditation techniques and allow to connect to higher sources of knowledge. Return to Source with this mudra. Similar to the "OK" gesture, touch your thumb and index fingers together to form an O, but keep your other three fingers completely straight and held together.

The **Hakini** mudra is another form that can be used to improve memory and concentration. It is very beneficial when used to access past life information and release karma. The hakini is also used to improve respiratory function. Spread the fingers of each hand apart and touch all your fingertips together.

The **Kalesvara** mudra is often recommended to calm the mind and body and help one release old negative thought patterns. Use this form to overcome addictions and patterns of abuse. Place both palms together pairing thumbs and all fingers at tips. Form a heart with your hands by folding the index, ring, and pinky fingers downward, with their last two phalanxes touching, and your thumbs pointing down. Point your middle, fire, fingers upwards with their tips touching.

The **Kapitthaka**, Elephant Apple Tree or Smiling Buddha mudra removes fear and brings happiness. This gesture is usually made in one of three positions: with your arms crossed over the chest, with the hand held up alongside either shoulder, or with the hands held palm upwards on the thighs. Extend your index and middle fingers and hold your pinky and ring fingers down with your thumb over them.

The **Kubera** mudra is called the "Make a Wish" mudra. Use this mudra with deep breathing exercise to center and align yourself to your soul purpose and desire, and then state your intentions or wishes several times out loud while you visualize their manifestation. Touch the tips of your thumb, index, and middle fingers together and tuck your ring finger and pinky your palm.

The **Linga** mudra helps bring spirit into the body, and can be used to create heat and improve circulation in the body. It is used most often to boost weakened immune systems and relieve bronchial issues. Weave the fingers of your hands together, point one thumb up and use your other thumb and index finger to circle the extended thumb. This form can be tiring if one is very weak, but will build up strength in the body when used regularly.

The **Mahasirs** mudra balances the mind and emotions with the harmonizing influence of earth energy. Use it to combat headaches, migraines and sinus issues. It is helpful when someone is experiencing stress combined with tears or sadness. Connect the thumb, index and middle fingers while holding your pinky straight and tucking the ring finger down into the palm near the thumb.

The **Mantangi** works with the solar plexus to release anger and resentment. Work with the Goddess Matangi to transmute your fire energy into peace and prosperity. Interlock the fingers on your hands together and point your middle fingers upward.

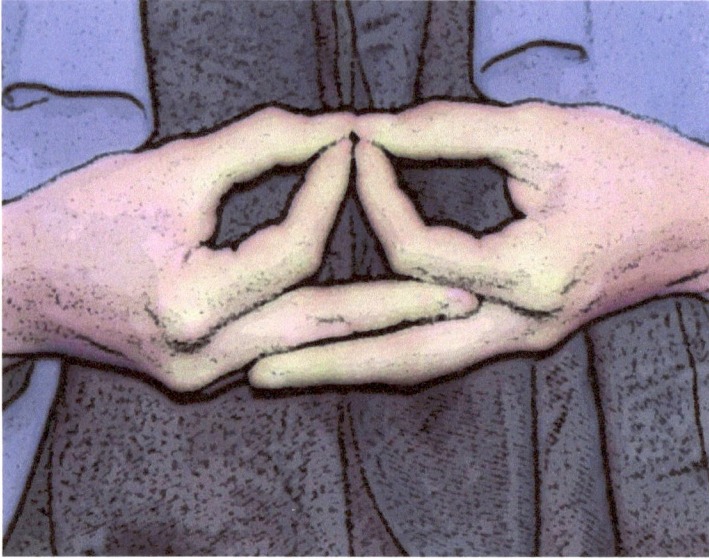

The **Mida-no Jouin** Mudra, or Dual Worlds pose, is a zen mudra used to see through the veil of illusion. The two hands mirror each other, showing the duality of enlightenment and illusion, truth and that which remains hidden. Cup your hands together to form a bowl in your lap, and then make two circles with your thumb and index fingers, with all four tips touching together. Use this pose when everyday reality is getting you down and you need to look past the details to see the bigger picture.

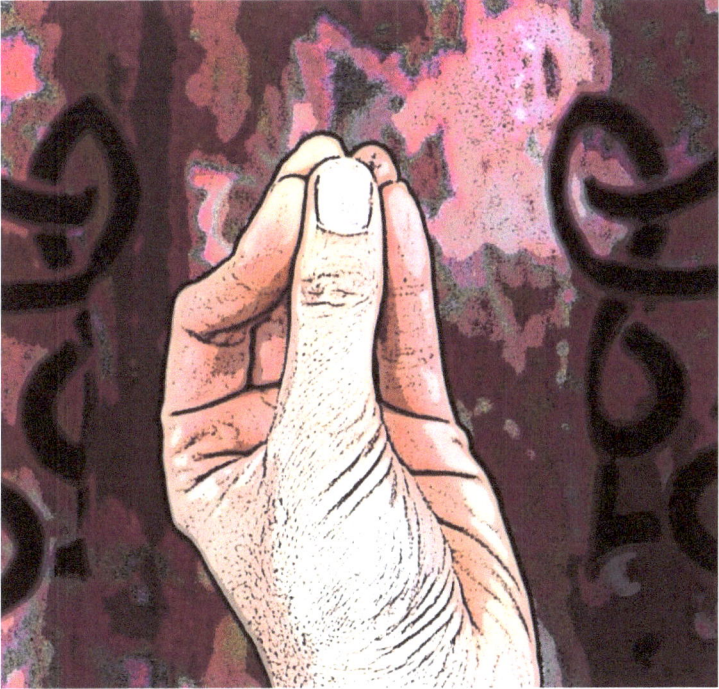

The **Mukula,** or **Samana,** mudra is used most often to instigate healing in the body. All five elements are brought together here to balance their energies and create harmony. With this mudra, energy takes form and creative energy can easily be directed to manifest with efficiency and purpose. Bring all five fingertips together and point upward for general meditation. In healing, place the fingertips of the part of the body that is needing healing or relief.

The **Mushti** mudra brings ether, or spirit, into form. It directs Qi energy into the body and aids in the detoxification process. Let go of stress, anger and aggression and claim your inner power. You are pure spirit in a divine physical form. Be well! Make a fist with your thumb folded to cover the ring and middle fingers.

The **Namaskara**, or **Anjali,** mudra is used to express respect, gratitude and good-will. Most often, it accompanies the "Namaste", an expression that signifies both a salutation and the idea that the light in me bows to light in you. With the hands held at chest level, it indicates a simple greeting, while the hands held higher at head level indicate profound respect or reverence.

The **Prana** mudra encourages the flow of Qi, or life force, through the body. It brings ether into the lower chakras and helps get the digestive and elimination systems moving while awakening the air (mind) and fire (energy) to improve lung functions. Touch the tips of your thumb, ring finger and pinky together while holding your forefinger and middle finger straight.

The **Prithvi,** or Earth, mudra strengthens the body and mind. It is very grounding and relaxing. Connect your thumb and ring finger while extending the other fingers while holding your palm at the knee. This mudra is often used to help weak constitutions or those suffering from insecurities.

The **Pushan** mudra is dedicated to the sun god and used to show that we appreciate all aspects of life – both the good, and the bad. The contrast is important, and one hand shows you are willing to receive blessings, while the other indicates the willingness to remain detached from those blessings. On your right hand, touch your thumb and first two fingers together. On your left hand your thumb, ring finger and pinky come together, while your forefinger connects to the ring finger on the other hand. Be easy, and flow with life.

The **Shankh** mudra, also called the Conch or Shell Mudra, is used as a sign of worship throughout India. It helps remove negativity and allow blessings. Grip your left thumb with your right hand, making a fist, and cup your left hand around the right fist. Then raise your right thumb and left forefinger together to create point, the tip of the conch shell, ready to blast away unconscious living and herald the divine.

The **Shunya** mudra is used in the treatment of all sorts of hearing disorders. In the west, we like to use it to open ourselves to messages from Spirit, encouraging channeling and communication with our spirit guides or higher self. Tuck your middle finger into your palm, held in place by your thumb, and extend your other three fingers.

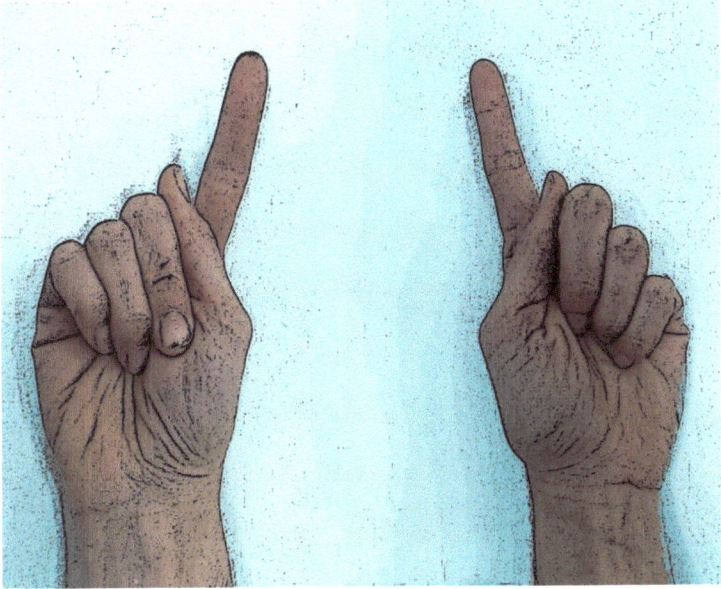

The **Suchi** Mudra is fantastic for children, especially high energy ones or those with behavioral issues. Give it a shot to subdue anger, violence, hyperactivity, or anxiety. Physically, it is often used to help with constipation. Make two fists and point upwards with your index fingers up over the head.

The **Surahi** Mudra balances all five elements (Ether, Air, Fire, Water, and Earth) and is considered one of the most powerful and effective mudras for healing and balancing the body, mind and soul. It brings all the meridians into harmony and allows one to be vibrationally aligned with their true self or soul. With your palms upward, extend your thumbs and connect your forefingers to the opposing middle fingers, while the ring fingers connect with the opposing pinkies.

The **Tarjani,** or **Karana,** Mudra is used to ward off evil and send away negative beings. Use it when you are feeling under psychic attack, or simply needing some protection and strength around you. As a general warding gesture, hold your hand at shoulder level with your palm facing outwards, and point your forefinger and pinky upwards while tucking your middle two fingers down under your thumb. To ward off a specific evil, point your fingers towards it to direct the energetic intent. This gesture is most often made with the left hand.

The **Ushas** mudra ushers in creative energy. Want to start
something new or get out of a rut? Try ushas. Want to start
a family, ushas is helpful here, too, helping with fertility and
the creative spark. The pose differs somewhat for men and
women: both intertwine their fingers together to form a
cup with the palms facing up. Women circle their right
thumb with their left thumb and forefingers, while men
simply place their right thumb on their left thumb.

The **Uttarabodhi** mudra is another gesture that children love to make. Hold your hands as in the Namaskara mudra and then fold down your middle, ring and little fingers so that they are interlocked. This gestures connects your crown chakra with your upper chakras so that your mind opens to Divine energy and soul communication from your higher self. It is believed to help usher in enlightenment and banish fear.

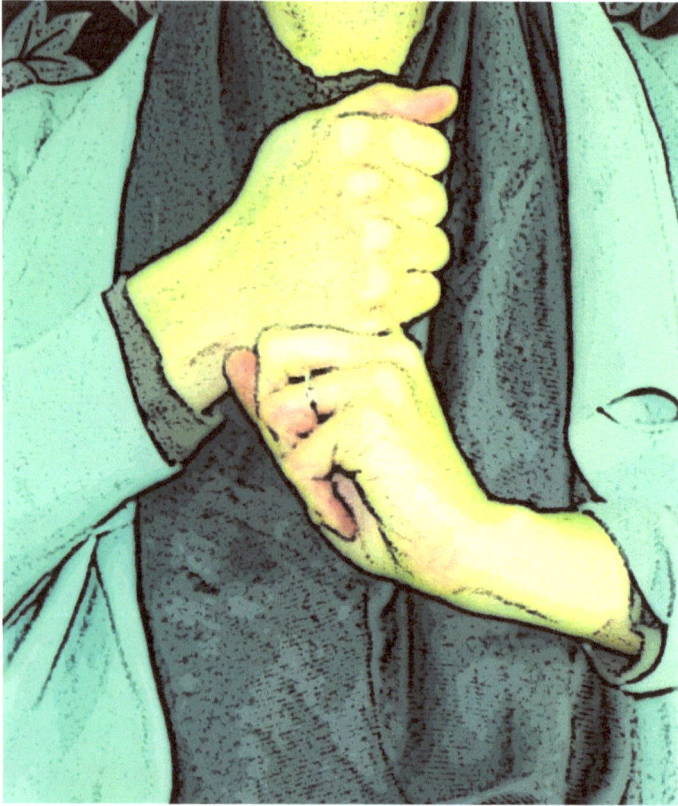

The **Vajra** mudra is used in Japan and Korea during Tantric meditation, and in Tibet to connect with the divine feminine. It brings the five elements into perfect union to enfold and protect the physical body, man, and is often used to help dispel the veil of illusion.

The **Varada** mudra presents an offering to the world. Give the gifts of compassion, generosity, liberation and peace to others by using this gesture. Here is the ascended master energies of Buddha and Christ, gifting all sentient beings with their grace and ascension. Hold your hand open and relaxed, palm up.

The **Yoni** Mudra invokes the creative energies of the divine feminine. Use this mudra to connect to a particular goddess, gather energy new endeavor or to benefit the sexual and reproductive organs. Form a diamond shape with your hand by connecting all your fingertips together, pointing your thumbs upward and your fingers downwards (the shape you form should be reminiscent of the vulva).

About the Author

Maya Cointreau has over 20 years of experience in vibrational healing. She is an Usui Reiki Master attuned in Karuna Reiki and the Iris Healing Method, along with having rigorously studied core shamanism, herbalism, flower essences, polarity therapy, naturopathic principles, homeopathy, crystal healing and aromatherapy. She co-owned and managed Hygeia, a holistic health and metaphysical wellness center for people, for five years and now owns and teaches through Enchanted Realms, a metaphysical center in New Milford, CT which opened in 2012. Her books are published by Earth Lodge™, a company specializing in vibrational healing remedies and publications for body, mind and spirit.

Visit her website at http://www.mayacointreau.com.

Namaste!